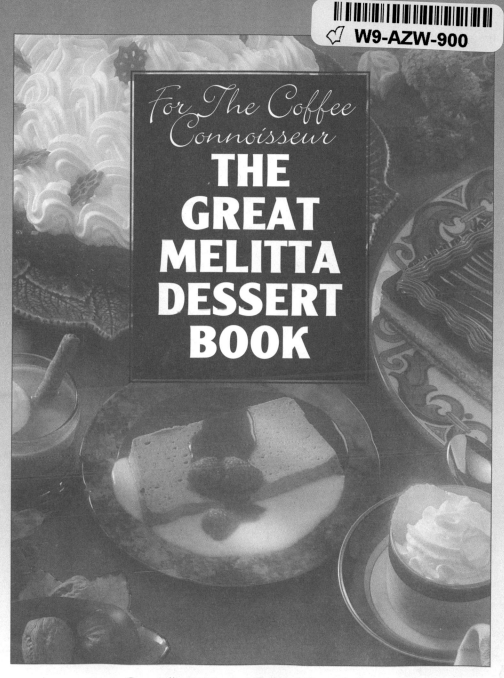

*For The Coffee Connoisseur*

# THE GREAT MELITTA DESSERT BOOK

Coordinated and Edited for Melitta
**By Barbara Hausner and
Irene Rothschild,** Certified Culinary Professional (CCP)

**MELITTA NORTH AMERICA, INC.**
**1401 BERLIN ROAD**
**P.O. BOX 900**
**CHERRY HILL, NJ 08003**

Manufactured in the United States of America

**ISBN 0-9642825-0-X**

First Printing, 1994

# Acknowledgements

This book acknowledges all the great chefs who created these recipes for great Melitta coffee. In particular, the Cappuccino Glacé, Mocha Macadamia Nut Tart, Chocolate Hazelnut Torte and Café Au Lait Cheesecake with Mocha Sauce are the names of some of the recipes developed by top pastry chefs in Philadelphia, South Jersey and Toronto. They participated in several consumer and VIP coffee dessert events at Hotel Atop The Bellevue in Philadelphia and Sutton Place in Toronto. Included were talented pastry chefs from The Four Seasons, Le Bec Fin, grano, The Rittenhouse and the Royal York Hotel, to name a few. At each event, the coffee desserts were not only beautiful, but delicious and elegant as well.

Also included in the book are some of Melitta's old favorites.

Here's a delectable sampling of recipes created exclusively for these Melitta dessert events. Enjoy. Bon Appetit!

**Editor's Note:** *Many of these recipes were created by chefs who have since moved on to other hotels, restaurants or culinary endeavors. Many of the recipes were altered or adapted for consumer use, uniformity and style.*

# THIS BOOK IS DEDICATED TO MELITTA BENTZ

If the entrepreneurial woman is a product of modern times, then Melitta Bentz was born a century too soon. It was at the beginning of the 20th century that Frau Bentz revolutionized the coffee industry by inventing and perfecting the "drip" method of coffeemaking, laying the groundwork for a business that continues to be a leader in the industry.

Melitta Bentz made her mark as a true "inventor" of her day. As a housewife from Dresden, Germany, born in 1873, she was frustrated by the traditional method of brewing coffee which called for boiling loose grounds or boiling grounds encased in a cloth bag. Either way, the brewed coffee was too cloudy, bitter and flawed by coffee grounds that too often found their way into the brew.

Frau Bentz experimented with the idea of "filtering" the coffee grounds to get a better quality coffee. She reasoned that by pouring water over the coffee grounds and through a filter, there would be less chance for the grounds and bitter oils to get into the brewed coffee. After testing a variety of "filters", she discovered that blotting paper, taken from the school notebook of her oldest son, worked very well. Cutting the paper into a disc, she placed it at the bottom of a perforated brass pot, measured in ground roasted coffee and poured hot water over the grounds. Perfectly filtered coffee - rich, full-bodied, without bitterness or grounds - dripped out of the bottom.

Melitta Bentz would not keep her discovery locked within the walls of her Dresden cottage. She received a patent registration on her invention on June 20, 1908. Shortly thereafter, she and her husband, Hugo, started a business and hired a tinsmith to produce the filter tops. The filter cone was technically improved and welded into a filter device made from brass. The "original filter cone" 13 cm high with a water dispersion device and inserted filter paper was complete. On December 15, 1908, the company M. Bentz was established. Within a year, they attended the Leipzig Trade Fair were they sold more than 1,200 "coffeemakers" - The Melitta company was born. By 1912, Melitta was manufacturing its own filters; stronger and more pure than the original blotting paper.

Managed by succeeding generations of Bentzs, the company continued the tradition of its founder. In 1937, the disc-shaped filter was replaced by the now familiar cone-shaped filter, which concentrates the grounds for more thorough saturation. Today, the metal top has given way to both porcelain and plastic filter tops which don't affect the flavor of the coffee.

The Melitta coffeemaker has maintained its popularity worldwide with its use in over 100 countries. Nearly three-quarters of US ground roast coffee drinkers enjoy the drip method.

Melitta Bentz shares a comraderie with other entrepreneurial women in history who devoted their energies to innovation.

# Contents

Preface
Notes on Ingredients
Notes on Techniques and Terms

## CAKES AND TORTES
Coffee Gingerbread
Café Melitta
Mocha Ecstasy
Marjolaine with Drambuie Crème Anglaise
Mocha Progrés
Mocha Fudge Cake
Café Au Lait Cheesecake with Mocha Sauce
White Chocolate Cheesecake
Chocolate Coffee Gateau with Pear Sabayon
Chocolate Espresso Torte
Brewster Mousse Cake
Chocolate Mocha Mousse Cake with Hazelnut Anglaise
Coffee Indulgence
Coffee Walnut Raspberry Torte
Chocolate Hazelnut Torte
Cappuccino Alla Zucca (Pumpkin Torte)

## COOKIES, BARS AND CREAM PUFFS
Biscotti di Café
Mocha Kisses
Mocha Spice Diamonds
Mini-Mocha Puffs
Mocha and Caramel Coffee Custard Puffs

## PIES, TARTS, CUSTARDS, MOUSSES AND FROZEN DESSERTS
Mocha Macadamia Nut Tart
Coffee and Sweet Chocolate Mousse Tart
Mocha Silk Pie
Mocha Sponge Custards
Poached Mocha Custards with Coffee-Roasted Bananas
Budino di Café
Cappuccino Glacé
Chilled Mocha Soufflé
Fat-Free Champagne and Coffee Mousse
English Trifle
Tiramisu

Double Coffee Granita
Sweetheart Coffee Mold

## QUICK AND EASY DESSERTS
Chilled Coffee Soufflé
Mocha Nut Cake
Coffee Custard Bruleé
Coffee Sponge Cake
Banana Flambé
Melitta Truffles
Melitta Nuggets
Creamy Coffee Fudge
Frozen Chocolate Cappuccino Mousse


## INTERNATIONAL COFFEES, FAVORITE COFFEE DRINKS AND DESSERT DRINKS
Espresso Coffee
Cappuccino
Chocolaccino
Spiced Coffee Vienna
Viennese Coffee Frost
Belgian Coffee
Irish Coffee
Latin Coffee El Salvador
Iced Coffee Rio
Minted Mocha Mist
Coffee Grog
Coffee Banana
Coffee De Cacao
Chilled Coffee A la Crème
Coffee Velvet
Monte Carlo
Crème de Café
Apricot Coffee Cream


## A GREAT CUP OF COFFEE
Coffee Brewing Tips

# PREFACE

Melitta coffee, which is an important ingredient in every recipe in this book, is top quality coffee, made using only the best Arabica coffee beans. These coffee beans are grown around the world and hand-picked to assure the exact stage of perfect ripeness.

Here's a synopsis of the whole process: Immediately after being picked, the coffee cherries are washed to remove any foreign particles. These ripe cherries are then hulled mechanically with a huller that uses rotating rubber rolls to gently disengage the cherries' flesh.

Hulled cherries are kept in huge concrete tanks where they ferment for 24 to 48 hours. This process loosens the remaining flesh, while influencing the coffee's ultimate aroma.

A second washing removes all remaining flesh, leaving only the cherries' surrounding parchment skin. Melitta's double washing is a very important, controlled way of preparing coffee that prevents any chance of spoiling the beans.

After this second washing, the cherries are turned and dried on large patios and in mechanical driers.

Once the coffee beans make it to the manufacturing facility, Melitta has pre-set blends to insure that its various coffees consistently taste the same. So, as coffee will differ from crop to crop, Melitta selects from a number of types, making sure they always complement one another, making a well-balanced premium blend of consistent quality.

But it doesn't stop with the blending. Melitta coffee is also expertly roasted, and then ground to a specified extra-fine grind. The fine grind achieves the fullest coffee flavor possible by not obstructing the flow of water through the filter during the brewing process.

So whether you're drinking or baking with Melitta coffee, you can always rest assured that your brew is the best quality, expertly cared for from the coffee bean to your cup, or, in honor of this book, your coffee cake! Bon Appetit!

# NOTES ON INGREDIENTS

**BUTTER** - Unsalted butter is preferable in baking. If using salted butter, reduce the amount of salt in the recipe.

**CHOCOLATE** - The four types of dark chocolate used most often for baking or desserts are semi-sweet, bittersweet, extra-bittersweet and unsweetened. Semi-sweet, bittersweet and extra-bittersweet may usually be used interchangeably. Semi-sweet is the sweetest, bittersweet is next, and extra-bittersweet is the least. The amount of sweetness may vary according to the manufacturer, and should be used according to your individual taste.

To make a chocolate less sweet (i.e. bittersweet or extra-bittersweet), substitute a small portion of unsweetened chocolate for the sweetened amount called for in the recipe.

Unsweetened chocolate contains no sugar and is made of pure chocolate liquor. It is sometimes referred to as "bitter" chocolate.

**COCOA** - Use unsweetened, preferably Dutch-processed.

**CREAM** - For whipping, use "heavy cream" or "whipping cream". Keep chilled until ready to whip.

**EGGS** - All recipes in this book call for "large" eggs unless otherwise specified. Changing the size of the eggs can alter the end product. Eggs will whip better if they are kept at room temperature for an hour.

**VANILLA BEANS** - When using vanilla beans steeped in a liquid, they may be rinsed and dried, and reused or placed in a container of sugar to make vanilla sugar. Two to three teaspoons of vanilla extract may be substituted, but should be added at the end of cooking time.

# NOTES ON TECHNIQUES

### COFFEE:
**Brewed** - Prepare as indicated on page 88, using 2 teaspoons ground Melitta Premium coffee per 3/4 cup (6 ounces) water. Please note that less coffee is needed when brewing Melitta coffee. For extra-strong coffee, use 1/2 cup (4 ounces) water.

**Ground** - Use freshly ground Melitta Premium coffee as is.

**Reduced** - Reheat regular strength coffee in a small saucepan on medium-high heat until reduced by about half unless otherwise specified.

**DRY INGREDIENTS** - Accurate measurements are important in baking. Stir ingredients, then spoon loosely into dry measuring cups. Level off with a spatula or the back of a knife.

**MELTING CHOCOLATE** - Chop chocolate coarsely and place in a dry bowl, measuring cup or saucepan. Melt slowly over very low heat, in a double boiler or bowl over hot water, or in a microwave, stirring occasionally until dissolved.

Milk chocolate or white "chocolate" contain milk solids and tend to burn more readily. It is best to melt slowly in a double boiler or in a bowl over hot water, stirring often.

**SCALDING** - Heat gently in a heavy saucepan until tiny bubbles just start to form around the edges of the pan.

# CAKES AND TORTES

# ENJOY YOUR JUST "DESSERTS"

Americans love dessert. And living in the great melting pot of world cultures has allowed us to adopt and combine international dessert traditions. Here are some facts about those gooey, sweet, chocolate, fruity concoctions.

- The "American" apple pie was actually invented in England.

- Americans did invent the Devil's Food Cake, a dark, chocolate contrast to the white Angel Food Cake.

- In Latin, chocolate is theobroma, "food of the gods".

- German chocolate cake wasn't invented in Germany, it owes its origin to an American man named German.

- Honey cake is eaten on the Jewish New Year with hopes of a year that is sweet.

- Cheesecakes were eaten by the ancient Greeks.

- In India, sweet puddings and cakes are flavored with rosewater, honey and nuts.

- The largest ice-cream sundae was one weighing 54,914 lbs. 3 oz., made in Alberta, Canada on July 24, 1988. It consisted of 44,689 lbs. 8 oz. of ice cream, 9,688 lbs. 2 oz. of syrup and 537 lbs. of topping.

- In Japan and China, desserts are not served with a meal. Meals conclude with fruit and tea. Dessert-type sweets are eaten as snacks.

- Every October for more than 80 years, the world's largest pumpkin pie is baked at the Circleville, Ohio Pumpkin Show. The pie weighs 350 pounds and measures 5 feet in diameter.

- As refined sugar and flour became readily available in Europe during the 18th and 19th centuries, desserts became more elaborate than ever. At European court banquets, dessert would include an array of creams, tarts, fruits, cakes, pastries, puddings, jellies and meringues.

- Lemon meringue pie was extremely fashionable among the wealthy of New York and Philadelphia in the mid to late 1800s.

- In France and Britain, the sweet dessert course is followed by yet another course consisting of nuts, fruit, cheese and dessert wines.

- In 1933, Mrs. Ruth Wakefield, owner of the Tollhouse Inn in Massachusetts, was in a hurry to bake some cookies. She chopped the chocolate instead of melting it, thus giving birth to the chocolate chip cookie. Nestle later bought the rights to the recipe.

- Many believe that gingerbread men were invented by Queen Elizabeth I of England.

- Flan, a baked caramel custard, is the dessert of choice in Spain, Portugal and Latin American countries.

- George Washington's favorite dessert was Martha's sugar cookies.

- The first brownie recipe was published in the Sears, Roebuck catalog in 1897.

- The longest banana split ever created measured 4.55 miles in length, and was made by residents of Selinsgrove, Pennsylvania on April 30, 1988.

Like every red-blooded American, just reading this is probably making you feel like brewing a rich pot of coffee and settling in with your favorite sweet sensation. Sinful?? Ask Shakespeare. He would respond, "If sack and sugar be a fault, God help the wicked."

Source:
The Great American Dessert Cookbook, Andrea Chesman and Fran
   Raboff, 1990, The Crossing Press, Freedom, California
The Guinness Book of World Records, 1993, Edited by Peter Matthews
   Bantam Books, New York, NY
The New Encyclopedia Britannica, 1991 Encyclopedia Britannica, Inc., Chicago, IL
Henry IV, part I, William Shakespeare

# COFFEE GINGERBREAD

*3 cups sifted all-purpose flour*
*2 teaspoons baking powder*
*2 teaspoons ground cinnamon*
*1 1/2 teaspoons ground ginger*
*1 teaspoon salt*
*1 teaspoon ground nutmeg*
*1/4 teaspoon ground cloves*
*1 cup shortening*
*1/2 cup granulated sugar*
*1/2 cup packed brown sugar*
*2 eggs*
*1 teaspoon baking soda*
*1/2 cup boiling water*
*1/2 cup brewed Melitta Premium coffee*
*1 cup molasses*
*Whipped cream for garnish*

Sift together first 7 ingredients; set aside.

In large bowl with mixer at medium speed, beat shortening, granulated sugar and brown sugar until light and fluffy. Add eggs; beat until well blended.

In a small bowl, dissolve baking soda in boiling water. Stir in coffee and molasses.

Using mixer at low speed, beat dry ingredients alternately with molasses mixture until well blended. Pour batter into greased 13x9x2-inch baking pan.

Bake in a 350° oven for 45 minutes or until toothpick inserted in center comes out clean. Let cool and cut into squares. Serve with whipped cream. Makes 16 servings.

# CAFÉ MELITTA

By: **Lawrence Irvin**
Culinary Concepts

## Cake Layer:

*1 stick unsalted butter*
*7 large eggs*
*1 cup sugar*
*1 teaspoon vanilla extract*
*1 ¼ cups all-purpose flour*
*¼ teaspoon salt*

Melt butter and set aside. Beat eggs and sugar until doubled in volume. Add vanilla, fold in melted butter; then add flour and salt in three batches. Pour batter into a greased and floured 9-inch cake pan. Bake in a 350° oven for 20 to 30 minutes, or until a cake tester comes out clean.

## Crunchy Layers:

*1 cup blanched toasted almonds*
*1 cup blanched toasted hazelnuts*
*1 ½ tablespoons cornstarch*
*1 ¼ cups sugar*
*8 egg whites*
*½ teaspoon cream of tartar*
*¼ teaspoon salt*
*½ teaspoon almond extract*
*½ teaspoon vanilla extract*

Line baking sheets with parchment paper traced with three 9-inch circles. Finely chop nuts and combine with cornstarch and I cup of sugar.

Whip egg whites until frothy and add cream of tartar and salt. Gradually add remaining sugar and beat until stiff; add almond and vanilla extracts. In three portions, fold into nut mixture. Spread batter over prepared circles and bake in a 275° oven for 65 to 70 minutes or until dry to the touch. Cool in pans for 15 minutes. Loosen and remove.

## Coffee Buttercream:

*6 egg yolks*
*½ cup sugar*
*3 tablespoons ground Melitta Premium coffee*
*½ cup boiling water*
*1 pound unsalted butter, room temperature*
*1 teaspoon vanilla extract*
*3 tablespoons Kahlúa liqueur*

Blend egg yolks and sugar together. Dissolve coffee grounds in boiling water and let steep a few minutes. Strain and blend into yolks. Stir over boiling water until mixture coats the back of a spoon. Remove and let cool. Beat butter until creamy and add vanilla and Kahlúa. Gradually blend in egg yolk mixture until consistency of a buttercream.

## Coffee Chocolate Coating:

*1 pound unsalted butter*
*3 tablespoons ground Melitta Premium coffee*
*12 ounces semi-sweet chocolate, chopped*

Melt butter and dissolve coffee grinds. Add chocolate, stir until melted and strain.

## Assembly:

Cut cake layer horizontally into thirds. Cover bottom layer with thin coating of coffee buttercream and I crunchy layer. Repeat, alternating layers and coating each with buttercream. Cover top and sides of cake with remaining buttercream and chill about I hour. Pour coffee chocolate coating over and smooth around top and sides. Refrigerate.

# MOCHA ECSTASY

By: **Ellen Gray and Jan Sheldon**
A Slice of Heaven

### Chocolate Truffle Cake:

*1 pound extra-bittersweet chocolate, chopped*
*1 stick plus 2 tablespoons unsalted butter*
*4 eggs, room temperature*
*1 tablespoon sugar*
*1 tablespoon all-purpose flour*
*1 tablespoon Drambuie liqueur*

Line a 9-inch round cake pan with parchment or wax paper and grease lightly. Melt chocolate and butter over low heat, stirring until dissolved. Remove from heat and let cool.

In mixer, beat eggs and sugar about 5 minutes, until thick and light. Blend in flour and stir in cooled chocolate mixture and Drambuie. Pour into prepared pan and bake in a 375° oven for 20 minutes or until set. Let cool on a rack; then place in freezer until firm. To remove from pan, place over gas or electric burner for a few moments until cake is loosened. Turn out onto a cardboard circle or serving dish.

### Chocolate Triple Threat Cake:

*1 ¼ ounces unsweetened chocolate, chopped*
*¾ cup plus 1 ½ tablespoons all-purpose flour*
*¾ teaspoon baking soda*
*Pinch salt*
*3 tablespoons unsalted butter, room temperature*
*¾ cup plus 1 ½ tablespoons dark brown sugar, firmly packed*
*1 large egg, room temperature*
*1 ¼ ounces unsweetened chocolate*
*2 ½ tablespoons buttermilk*
*⅓ cup boiling water*
*1 teaspoon strong brewed Melitta Premium coffee*

Line a 9-inch round cake pan with parchment or wax paper; grease and sprinkle with flour, shaking out excess. Melt chocolate in a double boiler over barely simmering water or in a microwave and let cool to lukewarm. Sift together flour, baking soda and salt and set aside.

In an electric mixer, beat butter and brown sugar until light and fluffy. Add egg; then melted chocolate blending well. Add dry ingredients alternately with buttermilk. Stir in boiling water and coffee and pour into prepared pan. Bake in a 375° oven for 25 minutes or until cake tester comes out clean. Let cool on rack.

## Chocolate Ganache:

*1 cup heavy cream*
*10 ounces bittersweet or semi-sweet chocolate, chopped*
*1 tablespoon strong brewed Melitta Premium coffee*

Scald cream and remove from heat. Add chocolate and coffee stirring until smooth.

## Mocha Mousse:

*1 ½ pounds semi-sweet chocolate*
*1 tablespoon strong brewed Melitta Premium coffee*
*5 egg yolks*
*¼ cup sugar*
*¼ pound unsalted butter, melted*
*1 cup heavy cream, whipped stiff*

Melt chocolate and coffee over low heat. Let cool to lukewarm. Beat egg yolks with sugar until thick and blend in melted chocolate. Mixture will "seize". Add melted butter a little at a time, mixing well. Add whipped cream gradually and beat or fold until thick and creamy.

## Assembly:

Turn out Truffle Cake and peel off paper. Place on cake circle or plate and spread with 1/3 of the mousse. Turn out Triple Threat layer cake and peel off paper. Split in half horizontally and place one sliced layer atop mousse. Spread with second 1/3 of the mousse and top with other half of Triple Threat layer. Cover top and sides of cake with remaining mousse. Smooth with a spatula and chill until firm. Set on a rack and pour ganache over the cake covering it completely. Chill again until set. Garnish with whipped cream rosettes and chocolate coffee beans, if desired.

# MARJOLAINE WITH DRAMBUIE CRÈME ANGLAISE

By: **Tom Heck**
  Ciboulette

## Marjolaine Cake Layers:

*1 ½  cups (6 ounces) blanched sliced almonds*
*1 cup (4 ounces) blanched hazelnuts*
*¾  cup sugar*
*2 tablespoons all-purpose flour*
*Pinch salt*
*⅞  cup (8) egg whites*
*¼  cup sugar*

Toast nuts to a golden brown and place in a food processor with 3/4 cup sugar. Finely grind together, pour into a bowl and mix with flour and salt.  Set aside.

Place egg whites in a mixer and whip to soft peaks.  Add remaining 1/4 cup sugar and beat until stiff but not dry.  Fold in nut mixture and spread onto two 10 1/2- x 15 1/2-inch jelly roll pans, lined with parchment paper.  Place in a 375° oven until lightly browned and not tacky to the touch.

## Ganache:

*¾  cup heavy cream*
*⅛ - ¼  cups strong brewed Melitta Premium coffee*
*6 ounces extra bittersweet chocolate, chopped*

Combine heavy cream and coffee and bring to a boil.  Pour over chocolate, stirring until chocolate is melted.  Set aside and let cool.

## Buttercream Filling:

*½ cup water*
*1 cup sugar*
*3 egg whites*
*2 sticks plus 2 tablespoons unsalted butter*
*2 teaspoons vanilla extract*
*1 teaspoon almond extract*
*1 cup blanched toasted almonds, coarsely ground*

Combine water and sugar in a small saucepan and bring to a boil. Cook undisturbed until sugar syrup reaches the firm ball stage (245°). Whip egg whites on high speed to soft peaks and add hot sugar syrup in a thin stream beating until cooled. Reduce speed and add butter, bit by bit until well blended. Divide mixture in half, adding vanilla extract to one half and the almond extract and chopped almonds to other half.

## Assembly:

Remove cake layers from pans and slice each in half lengthwise. Spread one layer with almond buttercream. Place second layer on top and spread with some ganache. Top with third layer and spread with vanilla buttercream. Top with remaining layer and chill cake 30 minutes. Trim edges, if desired, and coat sides with some more ganache. Using a squeeze bottle or a pastry bag with a star tip, use remaining ganache to decorate the top with "squiggles" or rosettes. To serve, cut into triangles, squares or rectangles and serve with Drambuie Crème Anglaise.

## Drambuie Crème Anglaise:

*2 1/4 cups milk*
*2 cups heavy cream*
*1/2 small vanilla bean*
*1/4 - 1/3 cup Drambuie*
*8 egg yolks*
*3/4 cup sugar*

Combine milk and heavy cream in a small saucepan. Split vanilla bean in half, scrape seeds and add both to pot. Add Drambuie to taste and bring to a boil.

In a mixer, beat egg yolks and sugar. Gradually stir in some of the hot milk mixture to warm the egg yolks and return the entire mixture to the pot. Cook over low heat until it coats the back of a spoon. Remove from heat, strain and cool.

# MOCHA PROGRÉS

By: **Marianne Laird**
   Le Bec Fin

## Meringue Layers:

*5 egg whites*
*1 cup sugar*
*3/4 cup ground hazelnuts*
*3/4 cup confectioners sugar*
*1 tablespoon coffee flavored milk\**

   Whip egg whites and 1/2 cup sugar on medium speed to firm peaks. Add remaining sugar on high speed for about 20 seconds. Combine hazelnuts and confectioners sugar and fold in along with coffee flavored milk.

   Place parchment paper onto baking sheets and mark with two 8-inch circles. Spread meringue into the circles and bake in a 275° oven for 1 hour, or until done. Let cool completely.

## \* Coffee flavored milk:

*1/4 cup milk*
*6 tablespoons ground Melitta Premium coffee*

   Scald milk, stir in coffee and let steep 5 minutes. Strain and let cool.

## Mocha Buttercream:

*2/3 cup egg whites*
*1 cup sugar*
*1 pound unsalted butter, room temperature*
*Coffee extract\**

Put egg whites and sugar into a bowl or in top of a double boiler and stir over barely simmering water until warm and sugar is dissolved. Remove and beat on medium high speed to firm peaks. Reduce speed and add butter, bit by bit until light and fluffy. Add coffee extract to taste.

## * Coffee Extract:

*¹/₂  cup Melitta Premium coffee, ground*
*¹/₄  cup boiling water*

Pour boiling water over coffee, stir, and let steep 5 minutes. Strain and let cool.

## Glaze:

*¹/₂  cup heavy cream*
*16 ounces milk chocolate, chopped*

Bring heavy cream to a boil and pour over chopped chocolate. Stir until melted. Let cool completely.

## Assembly:

*1 cup chopped hazelnuts*

Place one layer of meringue on bottom and spread with 1/4 to 1/2 inch mocha buttercream. Top with second meringue and cover top and sides with remaining buttercream. Chill until firm. Spoon cooled glaze over and chill until set. Dust sides with chopped hazelnuts.

# MOCHA FUDGE CAKE

by: **Richard Bookbinder**
15th Street Bookbinders Seafood House

*1 pound semi-sweet chocolate, chopped*
*1 pound unsalted butter, cut-up*
*1 cup granulated sugar*
*1 cup brewed Melitta Premium coffee, hot*
*8 large eggs*
*Whipped cream*

Slowly heat chocolate, butter, sugar and coffee, stirring until chocolate is melted. Remove from heat and pour into a mixer bowl. Whisk eggs together and slowly add to chocolate. Beat on low speed until blended. Pour into a 9-inch springform pan lined with aluminum foil and buttered. Bake in a 350° oven about 1 hour until almost set. Remove from oven and let cool. Refrigerate until firm. Garnish with whipped cream as desired.

# CAFÉ AU LAIT CHEESECAKE WITH MOCHA SAUCE

By: **Midi Bernadin**
  Metropolis Restaurant

*3 pounds cream cheese, room temperature*
*1 ½ cups granulated sugar*
*¼ cup cornstarch*
*1 teaspoon ground cinnamon*
*5 whole eggs*
*2 egg yolks*
*½ cup brewed Melitta Premium coffee*
*¾ cup heavy cream*

## Garnish:

*1 cup heavy cream*
*1-2 tablespoons confectioners sugar*
*1 tablespoon brewed Melitta Premium coffee, cooled*
*Chocolate shavings*
*Mocha Sauce (chocolate sauce thinned with Melitta coffee)*

In mixer, beat the cream cheese and sugar together until smooth and blended. Add the cornstarch and cinnamon, scraping sides of bowl with a rubber spatula.

Whisk or beat the eggs and yolks until light and lemon colored and fold into the cream cheese mixture. Blend in cooled coffee and heavy cream and pour mixture into a 9 or 10-inch deep cake pan. Place in a larger pan of hot water and bake in a 225° oven about 1½ hours or until firm in center. Remove from oven and let cool completely.

Whip cream to soft peaks and add confectioners sugar and coffee. Unmold cake, turn upside down and top with whipped cream. Sprinkle with chocolate shavings and serve with Mocha Sauce, if desired.

# WHITE CHOCOLATE COFFEE CHEESECAKE

*1 ¹/₂ cups chocolate wafer crumbs*
*6 tablespoons butter, melted*
*2 tablespoons sugar*
*2 (8 ounce) packages cream cheese, softened*
*1 cup sugar*
*3 eggs*
*8 ounces white chocolate, chopped*
*¹/₄ cup heavy cream*
*1 cup sour cream*
*¹/₂ cup strong brewed Melitta Premium coffee, cooled*
*1 tablespoon cornstarch*
*Whipped cream and coffee bean candies for garnish.*

Preheat oven to 325°. In medium bowl, combine crumbs, butter and sugar. Press mixture on bottom and two-thirds up the sides of a 9-inch springform pan. Bake 10 to 15 minutes or until browned. Cool on rack.

In large bowl with mixer at medium speed, beat cream cheese and sugar until light and fluffy. Add eggs, one at a time, beating well after each addition.

In small saucepan over low heat, heat chocolate and cream until melted, stirring often.

Using low speed, gradually beat melted chocolate, sour cream, coffee and cornstarch into cream cheese mixture until just combined.

Pour batter into baked crust. Bake 60 to 70 minutes or until outer 2" of cake is firm and slightly puffed (center will be nearly set when shaken). Cool on rack to room temperature (about 4 hours).

Cover with plastic wrap. Refrigerate at least 12 hours. Before unmolding cake, use spatula to loosen crust from pan. Garnish with whipped cream and coffee bean candies. Makes 12 servings.

# CHOCOLATE COFFEE GATEAU WITH PEAR SABAYON

By: **Teresa M. Wall**
Café Nola

## Chocolate Coffee Gateau:

*12 ounces imported bittersweet chocolate, chopped*
*1 1/2 sticks unsalted butter*
*1 teaspoon espresso powder*
*1/4 cup strong brewed Melitta Premium coffee*
*9 large eggs, separated*
*1 1/4 cups sugar*
*1/4 cup fine ground Melitta Premium coffee*
*1/2 cup finely ground nuts* (macadamia, hazelnuts, etc.)
*1 teaspoon ground cinnamon*
*2 tablespoons coffee liqueur* (optional)
*Granulated sugar*
*Confectioners sugar*

Melt chocolate and butter and set aside. Dissolve espresso powder in brewed coffee and let cool.

Beat egg yolks with sugar until thick and light. Blend in coffee granules, nuts, cinnamon, reserved coffee, and coffee liqueur, if using. Add slightly cooled chocolate.

Beat egg whites until stiff but not dry. Fold into chocolate mixture and pour into a 10-inch springform pan that has been buttered and sprinkled with sugar. Bake in a 275° oven for 1 1/2 hours. Serve dusted with confectioners sugar and dollops of Pear Sabayon.

## Pear Sabayon:

*5 egg yolks*
*¹/₂ cup sugar*
*¹/₄ cup pear poaching liquid or nectar*
*2 tablespoons Poire William liqueur*
*1 ¹/₄ cups heavy cream*

In a metal bowl over boiling water or in top of a double boiler, whisk egg yolks, sugar, pear liquid and Poire William liqueur together until mixture thickens, 5 to10 minutes. Remove from heat and whisk over ice water until cool. Whip cream to soft peaks and fold in. Refrigerate until ready to serve.

# CHOCOLATE ESPRESSO TORTE

By: **Locke Johnson**
   **Christine Stucki**
   The Museum Catering Company

## Cake:

*7 ounces semi-sweet chocolate, chopped*
*2 sticks unsalted butter, cut-up*
*1/2 cup strong brewed Melitta Premium coffee*
*2 tablespoons coffee liqueur, optional*
*8 eggs, separated*
*1 cup sugar*
*1/3 cup cake flour, sifted*

Melt chocolate and butter together. Mix in coffee and liqueur, if using. Stir in egg yolks, 1/2 cup sugar, and cake flour until well blended.

Beat egg whites adding remaining sugar gradually until stiff peaks form. Fold into chocolate mixture and turn batter into a 10 1/2- x 15 1/2-inch sheet pan that has been lined with parchment paper. Bake in a 325° oven 25 to 30 minutes. Cool completely.

## Filling:

*1 cup heavy cream*
*1 teaspoon sugar*
*2 1/2 tablespoons ground Melitta Premium coffee*
*1/2 tablespoon strong brewed Melitta Premium coffee*

Whip cream and sugar until it starts to thicken. Add coffee grinds and liquid coffee and beat to soft peaks.

## Glaze:

*4 tablespoons unsalted butter*
*4 ounces semi-sweet chocolate, chopped*

Melt chocolate and butter in a bowl or a double boiler over warm water blending well.

## Assembly:

Turn out cake and remove parchment.  Slice in half horizontally, spread filling on one layer and cover with second layer.  Top with chocolate glaze.  Let harden before cutting. Makes 12-15 servings.

# BREWSTER MOUSSE CAKE

By: **Pamela Green & Gerard Gehin**
    Beau Rivage

## Chocolate Cake:

*2 cups all-purpose flour*
*2 cups sugar*
*³/₄ cup cocoa powder*
*1 teaspoon salt*
*2 teaspoons baking soda*
*2 large eggs*
*2 teaspoons vanilla extract*
*1 cup milk*
*1 cup brewed Melitta Premium coffee, cooled*
*¹/₂ cup oil*

Line a 10-inch round cake pan with parchment or wax paper and grease.

Sift together dry ingredients into a mixer bowl. Combine eggs, vanilla, milk, coffee and oil and blend into dry ingredients. Beat in a mixer on medium speed for 1 minute. Scrape down and mix again for 15 to 20 seconds. Pour batter into prepared pan and bake in a 350° oven for 15 to 20 minutes. Cool on rack, turn out and remove paper. Line the bottom of a 10-inch springform pan with the whole cake layer, or half of the layer sliced horizontally and reserve the remaining half for another use.

## Brewster Custard Mousse:*

*¹/₄ cup brewed Melitta Premium coffee*
*¹/₄ cup coffee liqueur*
*5 teaspoons unflavored gelatin*
*³/₄ cup heavy cream*
*5 egg yolks*
*³/₄ cup sugar*
*2 cups heavy cream*

Combine cooled coffee and coffee liqueur and sprinkle gelatin over to soften. Heat to dissolve and let cool.

Heat 3/4 cup heavy cream to scalding. In mixer, beat egg yolks and sugar on high speed until thick and a ribbon forms when beater is lifted. Gradually add hot cream and return to saucepan. Cook on medium low heat until mixture thickens and coats the back of a spoon. Stir in coffee and gelatin mixture blending well. Pour into a bowl and place over larger bowl of ice and water to cool. Stir occasionally until mixture starts to set.

Whip 2 cups heavy cream to soft peaks and fold into custard. Spoon or pipe with a pastry bag and plain tip onto the chocolate cake base. Chill 5-6 hours or overnight to set. Run a warmed knife around edge and unmold. Garnish with whipped cream rosettes and candy coffee beans.

*Editor's Note: Brewster is the name of Melitta's larger-than-life, friendly filter cone mascot.*

# CHOCOLATE MOCHA MOUSSE CAKE WITH HAZELNUT AGLAISE

By: **Shawn Sollberger**
   SFUZZI

*1 pound semi-sweet chocolate, melted*
*6 large eggs*
*1 cup sugar*
*1 cup heavy cream*

   Melt chocolate and set aside. Beat eggs and sugar together until double in volume. Blend in cooled melted chocolate. Whip cream and fold in. Pour into a 10-inch springform pan. Cover outside tightly with foil and bake in a water bath in a 325° oven for 45 minutes. Remove and let cool on a rack. Remove sides and let cake cool completely.

## Mousse:

*7 ounces semi-sweet chocolate*
*2 tablespoons unsalted butter*
*2 eggs, separated*
*1 ½ tablespoons Kahlúa*
*1 tablespoon reduced coffee*
*1 cup heavy cream*
*¼ cup sugar*

   Melt chocolate and butter together over low heat and let cool to room temperature. Whisk in egg yolks; then Kahlúa and coffee. Whip cream to soft peaks and fold in. Whip egg whites with 1/3 of the sugar to soft peaks. Add remaining sugar and fold into the chocolate mixture. Chill until thick.

## Assembly:

*White chocolate shavings, optional*
*Chopped hazelnuts, optional*

Slice cake in half horizontally and cover bottom layer with 1 inch of the mousse. Place remaining cake half on top and chill until set. Spread remaining mousse over top and sides of cake. Garnish as desired with rosettes and white chocolate shavings on top and chopped toasted hazelnuts on sides. Serve with Hazelnut Anglaise.

## Hazelnut Anglaise:

*3 egg yolks*
*1/4 cup sugar*
*1 cup milk*
*1/2 tablespoon Frangelico*

Whisk egg yolks and sugar in a double boiler or in a bowl over hot water until thick and light. Bring milk to scalding and add to eggs, continuing to whisk until thick. Remove from heat, add Frangelico and let cool.

# COFFEE INDULGENCE

by: **Amy Bause Barta**
Symphony Inc.

## Coconut Meringue:

*1/3 cup confectioners sugar*
*2 tablespoons all-purpose flour*
*1/2 cup grated coconut*
*3 egg whites*
*1/4 cup sugar*

Sift confectioners sugar and flour together and combine with coconut. Whip egg whites to soft peaks. Gradually beat in sugar until stiff peaks form. Fold in coconut mixture. Line a baking sheet with parchment paper and draw an 8-inch circle. Pipe or spread meringue into the circle and bake in a 325° oven for 1 hour.

## Coffee Bavaroise:

*2 teaspoons unflavored gelatin*
*1 1/2 cups milk*
*1/2 cup ground Melitta Premium coffee*
*4 egg yolks*
*3/4 cup granulated sugar*
*1 1/2 cups heavy cream*

Soften gelatin in 1/4 cup cold milk. Bring remaining milk to a boil, add coffee and let steep 5 minutes. Strain through cheesecloth or a fine strainer.

Blend egg yolks and sugar, whisking until smooth. Slowly add 1/2 cup of the steeped milk. Return to the remaining milk in saucepan and reheat, stirring until mixture lightly coats the back of a spoon. Be careful not to boil. Remove from heat and stir in softened gelatin. Pour into a bowl and cool in refrigerator or over ice water, stirring occasionally until mixture starts to thicken. Whip cream to soft peaks and fold in.

## Bitter Chocolate Ganache:

*½ cup heavy cream*
*2 tablespoons sugar*
*2 tablespoons unsalted butter*
*½ cup chopped unsweetened chocolate*

Combine cream, sugar and butter and bring to a boil. Place chocolate in a bowl and pour mixture over, stirring well until completely melted. Let cool.

## Assembly:

*1 package ladyfingers*

Line a 9-inch springform pan with ladyfingers. Trim coconut meringue to fit inside and pipe or spoon a thin layer of chocolate ganache on top. Fill mold with coffee bavaroise and refrigerate until set. When completely chilled, glaze the cake with melted remaining ganache, if desired. Unmold to serve.

# COFFEE WALNUT RASPBERRY TORTE

**By: Michael A. Campbell**
   Magee Hospital

## Cake:

*8 ounces shortening*
*1 ½ cups dark brown sugar*
*6 large eggs*
*½ cup sugar*
*½ teaspoon salt*
*1 teaspoon vanilla extract*
*2 cups strong brewed Melitta Premium coffee*
*3 ¼ cups all-purpose flour*
*¼ cup cocoa powder*
*1 teaspoon baking soda*
*1 teaspoon baking powder*
*⅔ cup chopped walnuts*
*2 tablespoons rum*

Heat shortening and dark brown sugar, stirring until melted. Set aside. Beat eggs, sugar, salt and vanilla until light and fluffy. Blend in melted shortening and 1/2 cup coffee. Sift together dry ingredients and stir in with nuts. Pour into two greased or parchment-lined 15½- x 17½-inch sheet pans and bake in a 350° oven for 20 minutes. Cool 5 minutes and turn out onto wax paper. Remove parchment, if using. Combine remaining 1½ cups coffee with rum and brush over cakes.

## Filling:

*6 tablespoons shortening*
*$^1/_4$ teaspoon salt*
*$^1/_2$ teaspoon vanilla extract*
*6 cups (1 $^1/_2$ pounds) confectioners sugar*
*$^1/_4$ cup water*

Combine all ingredients and beat until smooth, 5 to 10 minutes.

## Frosting:

*$^1/_2$ cup ground Melitta Premium coffee*
*4 cups heavy cream*
*2 pounds semi-sweet chocolate, chopped*
*$^1/_2$ cup chopped walnuts*

Wrap and tie coffee in cheesecloth and place in a saucepan with heavy cream. Bring to a boil, remove and squeeze liquid from cheesecloth back into saucepan. Add chocolate, stirring until melted. Remove 2 cups and add walnuts. Set aside to cool. Whip remaining mixture until frosting consistency.

## Assembly:

*24 ounces raspberry preserves*

Slice cakes in half lengthwise. Spread raspberry preserves on one piece and filling on another. Place the two pieces together so the fillings mix. Spread preserves over top and follow with another layer that has been spread with filling. Repeat using all layers and place in freezer for two hours. Slice the cake diagonally from upper right corner to lower. Turn the cake halves on their sides facing each other and push the two pieces together using a little of the extra buttercream. This will form a long triangle. Cover entire cake with frosting and drizzle chocolate and nut mixture over top.
Makes 20 - 24 servings.

# CHOCOLATE HAZELNUT TORTE

By: **Eddie Hales**
Four Seasons Hotel

*8 ounces hazelnuts, toasted and skinned*
*6 ounces semi-sweet chocolate, chopped fine*
*3 tablespoons candied orange peel, diced*
*6 egg yolks*
*½ cup sugar*
*4 egg whites*
*Chocolate Coffee Ganache\**

Put nuts, chocolate and orange peel in a food processor and chop very fine.

Beat egg yolks with 1/4 cup of sugar until thick and light. Fold in the nut mixture. Whip egg whites until frothy. Gradually add remaining 1/4 cup sugar and beat until stiff. Fold into the yolk mixture and pour into a 9-inch round cake pan that has been greased and lined with wax paper. Bake in a 350° oven for 25 to 30 minutes. Cool on rack; then unmold.

## *Chocolate Coffee Ganache:

*1 cup heavy cream*
*4 tablespoons unsalted butter*
*9 ounces semi-sweet chocolate, chopped*
*2 tablespoons triple strength brewed Melitta Premium coffee*

Bring heavy cream and butter to a boil and pour over the chopped chocolate. Stir until chocolate is melted and add the coffee. Let cool; then glaze cooled cake.

# CAPPUCCINO ALLA ZUCCA
## (Pumpkin Cappuccino Torte)

By: **Eric Boerner**
Adam's Mark Hotel

### Caribbean Spice Cake:

*1 1/4 cups light brown sugar*
*3 large eggs*
*1 1/2 cups all-purpose flour*
*1 1/4 tablespoons baking powder*
*Ground cinnamon*
*Grated or ground nutmeg*
*Grated or ground mace*
*Ground coriander*
*Ground cardamon*
*11 tablespoons unsalted butter, melted and cooled*
*2/3 cup heavy cream*

Beat brown sugar and eggs together until creamy and smooth. Sift together flour, baking powder and 4 teaspoons combined spices to taste and stir in. Add butter and cream and blend until smooth. Pour into a buttered and floured 10-inch springform pan and bake in a 350° oven for 30 minutes or until slightly firm in center. Let cool in pan and fill with Sweet Potato or Pumpkin Mousse. Unmold when set.

### Sweet Potato or Pumpkin Mousse:

*1/2 package unflavored gelatin*
*1/3 cup water*
*1 cup cooked sweet potato or pumpkin puree*
*3 tablespoons maple syrup*
*1 tablespoon Kahlúa*
*1/4 cup sweetened condensed milk*
*1/2 cup heavy cream*
*2 tablespoons Melitta coffee extract**

Soften gelatin in cold water and dissolve over hot water. Set aside. Combine sweet potato or pumpkin puree, maple syrup, Kahlúa and condensed milk. Mix until smooth and stir in gelatin mixture. Whip cream and coffee extract to soft peaks and fold in. Spoon over Caribbean Spice Cake, smoothing top. Chill until set. Unmold and serve slices with Caramel-Coffee Creme Anglaise, if desired.

## Caramel-Coffee Creme Anglaise:

*1 cup light cream*
*1/3 cup sugar*
*4 egg yolks*
*1/2 vanilla bean, split*
*3 tablespoons sugar*
*Melitta coffee extract\**

In a small heavy saucepan combine light cream and vanilla bean and bring to the scalding point. Let steep 10 to 15 minutes. Whisk or beat egg yolks with 1/3 cup sugar and gradually stir in warm cream. Return to the saucepan and cook on low heat, stirring until mixture thickens enough to coat the back of a spoon. Strain and cool over ice water, stirring occasionally, to room temperature. Set aside.

Heat a small saute pan and add remaining 3 tablespoons sugar. Cook on medium heat, shaking pan (do not stir) until sugar reaches medium amber color. Remove from heat and immediately stir in coffee extract to taste. Blend into custard.

*\*Brew 4 tablespoons ground Melitta Premium coffee in 1 cup Kahlúa. Strain and reduce by half. Stir in 2 tablespoons light corn syrup.*

# COOKIES, BARS AND CREAM PUFFS

# COFFEE HAS BEEN ENJOYED AROUND THE GLOBE THROUGH-OUT THE AGES

## The Brew Has Traveled a Cultural Journey From Male-Dominated Coffeehouses to Ladies Cafés

Relaxing with a cup of coffee is a daily ritual enjoyed by many people all over the world. And whether it's accompanied by breakfast before dawn or enjoyed as an afternoon pick-me-up on the weekend or after a good meal in the evening, coffee continues to grow in popularity.

Interestingly, for centuries coffee was only enjoyed away from home. It was a hot beverage that was celebrated and enjoyed in specially-designed coffee houses.

Many of these famous places, some of them more than 350 years old, still exist today. There is the famous Vienna Café "Central", a popular hang-out for writers, the Café "Greco" located in Rome, where German authors Goethe and Schopenhauer were frequent guests, or the Café "Aux Deux Magots" in Paris, where existentialists Jean-Paul Sartre and his companion Simone de Beauvoir lamented their theories of life.

## Coffeehouse Culture Traced to Africa

Europeans' coffeehouse culture can actually be tracked back as far as 1300 A.D. to Ethiopia. By 1500 the first coffeehouses were already present in Mecca. But only after the first coffeehouse in Constantinople (Istanbul today) opened in 1554, did word of the "black water" finally reach Europe.

A century later the first coffeehouses were opened in scenic trade and harbor cities like Venice in 1645, London in 1652, Marseille in 1659, The Hague and Amsterdam in 1663 and Hamburg in 1679.

In spite of much skepticism, opposition and prohibition in the mid to late 1600s, coffee became an instant success with the fun-loving aristocrats. Just a short while later, commoners also began enjoying coffee and they had no intention of being deprived of its pleasure, so they began cultivating their own coffeehouses beginning in Paris in 1675, Vienna in 1683, Leipzig in 1689 and Berlin in 1721.

## Coffeehouses were the Original Political, Cultural and Business Clubs in England

By the last quarter of the 18th century, there were thousands of coffeehouses in England. In fact, they were institutions which later evolved into the English political, cultural and business clubs of today. Their congenial atmospheres fostered lively and sometimes violent debates.

In England, there was a small minority who did not approve of these centers for the exchange of new ideas and viewed them with suspicion. Charles II sided with them and in 1775 issued a proclamation ordering all coffeehouses to close, claiming that they had produced "very evil and dangerous effects"...here diverse, false, malicious and scandalous reports are devised. The King's ban produced such a violent reaction, including threats of revolution against the monarch, that within a few days, Charles was forced to permit coffeehouses to reopen.

## Women Excluded from Coffee Enjoyment at First

Historically, women were banned from all public coffeehouses. But like men, they also wanted to take part in coffee enjoyment. So in the 18th century it became customary for ladies of the upper crust to invite each other to coffee rendezvous.

These rendezvous became daily or weekly afternoon social events where visitors were served in specially-decorated parlors. These parlors were off-limits to men so the ladies were free to indulge in their passion for coffee and to discuss female subjects undisturbed.

Men sneered at these socials and named them "Kaffee Klatsches" (gossip sessions). Needless to say, men were doing the same thing in their own guys-only coffeehouses.

It was not until the second half of the 19th century that women were finally permitted to drink coffee in public. However, they were still excluded from the coffeehouses. But eventually separate establishments called "cafés" were opened for them.

Today both cafés and coffeehouses are gaining popularity in many North American cities as people continue to drink less alcohol socially.

# BISCOTTI DI CAFÉ

By: **Lucia Ruggiero-Martello**
grano

*²/₃ cup blanched slivered almonds*
*3 tablespoons ground Melitta Premium coffee*
*2 tablespoons Kahlúa*
*1 stick unsalted butter, room temperature*
*³/₄ cup sugar*
*2 large eggs*
*2 cups plus 2 tablespoons all-purpose flour*
*1 ¹/₂ teaspoons baking powder*
*¹/₂ teaspoon salt*

Place almonds in a shallow pan and toast in a 350° oven for 7 to 8 minutes, until golden brown. Set aside. Heat ground coffee and Kahlúa together.

Cream butter and sugar until light and fluffy. Beat in eggs, one at a time; add coffee and Kahlúa mixture. Combine flour, baking powder and salt, and add on low speed until blended. Stir in nuts. Divide dough in half and roll into 2 logs about 2 inches in diameter. Place on a greased and floured baking sheet and bake in a 325° oven for 25 minutes or until lightly browned. Remove to a rack and let cool for 5 minutes. Place on a cutting board and with a serrated knife slice diagonally about ¹/₂ inch thick. Place slices flat on the baking sheet and return to the oven for 10 minutes longer to toast. Let cool before serving. May be stored in airtight containers.
Makes 24.

# MOCHA KISSES

*½ cup unsalted butter, room temperature*
*⅔ cup pure cocoa*
*½ teaspoon vanilla extract*
*½ teaspoon black walnut extract*
*⅓ cup hot strong Melitta Premium coffee*
*4 cups confectioners sugar*
*¾ cup finely chopped pecans or hazelnuts (optional)*

In large bowl, combine butter, cocoa, vanilla and walnut extract. Then add coffee and one-half of sugar to bowl, continue to mix. Knead the remaining sugar and nuts into the mixture.

Place in freezer for 5 minutes or in refrigerator for 20 minutes. Using two teaspoons, drop on wax-papered tray. Cover with wax paper and refrigerate for a couple of hours or until ready to serve.

**Suggestion:** Roll in powdered sugar and/or shredded coconut.
Yields approximately 24 - 30 Mocha Kisses.

# MOCHA SPICE DIAMONDS

By: **Laura LaGue**
   Hyatt Hotel - Cherry Hill

*4 egg yolks*
*1 1/2 cups brown sugar*
*2 1/4 cups all-purpose flour*
*1 teaspoon salt*
*1 teaspoon baking powder*
*1/4 teaspoon ground cloves*
*1 teaspoon ground allspice*
*1 teaspoon cinnamon*
*1/2 cup double strength brewed Melitta Premium coffee, cooled*
*3/4 cup mini chocolate chips*
*1 cup chopped walnuts*
*1/4 cup unsalted butter, softened*
*1 cup sifted confectioners sugar*
*3 tablespoons double strength brewed Melitta Premium coffee*

Beat egg yolks and brown sugar until light and fluffy. Sift dry ingredients together and add to egg mixture alternately with 1/2 cup coffee. Stir in chocolate chips and walnuts and spread into a greased 9x13-inch pan. Bake in a 350° oven about 20 minutes or until golden.

Beat the softened butter and confectioners sugar together; add remaining coffee and spread on cookies while still warm. Let cool completely and cut into diamond shapes or squares.

# MINI-MOCHA PUFFS

by: **Denise Heisler**
Mont Serrat

## Puffs:

*8 ounces brewed Melitta Premium coffee*
*6 tablespoons unsalted butter*
*1 cup all-purpose flour*
*¼ teaspoon salt*
*4 eggs, room temperature*

In a medium-sized saucepan, bring coffee and butter to a boil. Remove from heat and add flour and salt all at once, stirring vigorously until dough forms a firm ball. Transfer to a mixer or food processor and add eggs one at a time until completely mixed. Drop by heaping tablespoons about 1 inch apart, onto a greased baking sheet. Place in a pre-heated 400° oven for 10 to 12 minutes; reduce to 350° and bake for 15 minutes longer or until golden brown. Remove from oven and place pan on rack to cool. Do not remove pastries from pan until cooled or they will deflate. Makes 12.

## Filling:

*6 egg yolks*
*1 scant cup sugar*
*1 ½ cups heavy cream*
*2 cups brewed Melitta Premium coffee*
*6 tablespoons cornstarch*
*1 tablespoon vanilla extract*
*4 tablespoons unsalted butter*
*3-4 ounces mini-chocolate chips*

In a medium-sized saucepan, combine egg yolks, sugar, cream, coffee and cornstarch and bring to a boil over medium heat, whisking constantly. Mixture must be brought to a boil and cooked for one minute after it thickens. Remove from heat and stir in vanilla extract and butter. Transfer to a bowl, cover and chill. Fold in chocolate chips.

## Topping:

*3 ounces mini-chocolate chips*
*6 ounces brewed Melitta Premium coffee*

Combine chocolate chips and coffee and place in a microwave oven. Heat 45 seconds on low power to melt chocolate. Stir well to form a thin syrup.

## Assembly:

Put filling into a pastry bag with a large plain tip and insert into side of pastry shells and fill. Or, cut puffs in half, spoon on some filling and replace tops. Drizzle with melted chocolate/coffee syrup.

# MOCHA AND CARAMEL COFFEE CUSTARD PUFFS

By: **Jake's**

## Filling:

*12 egg yolks*
*2 cups sugar*
*2 packages unflavored gelatin*
*¼ cup water*
*6 cups heavy cream*
*1 cup strong brewed Melitta Premium coffee*
*4 teaspoons vanilla extract*
*8 ounces semi-sweet chocolate, chopped*
*16 ounces caramel sauce*

Whisk egg yolks and sugar together in a large bowl. Add gelatin to cold water and let soften. Bring cream and coffee to a boil, remove from heat and gradually whisk into the yolk mixture. Return to saucepan and cook on low heat, stirring constantly until mixture coats the back of a spoon. Stir in softened gelatin to dissolve. Remove from heat and add vanilla. Divide mixture in half, adding chocolate to one half, and caramel sauce to the other. Refrigerate until set.

## Cream Puffs

*2 ¼ cups all-purpose flour*
*1 tablespoon sugar*
*½ tablespoon salt*
*Zest 1 orange*
*2 cups water*
*8 ounces unsalted butter, cut-up*
*6-7 eggs*

Combine flour, sugar, salt and orange zest in a bowl and set aside. Bring water and butter to a rolling boil. Remove from heat and stir in flour mixture. Return to heat and cook, stirring until mixture comes together and no longer sticks to side of pan. Transfer to a mixer or food processor and let cool about 5 minutes. Add eggs, one at a time, blending well after each. Using a spoon or pastry bag with a large tip, shape into puffs onto a greased baking pan. Bake in a 400° oven for 15 minutes; reduce to 325° and bake until dry about 1 hour longer.

Cut puffs at top third to form a lid. Remove any soft dough from center and fill with a layer of chocolate and coffee caramel custards.

## Chocolate Glaze:

*8 ounces semi-sweet chocolate, chopped*
*2 tablespoons light corn syrup*
*1 cup heavy cream*
*1 tablespoon orange liqueur* (optional)

Place chocolate and corn syrup in a small bowl. Bring cream and liqueur to a boil. Pour over chocolate and stir until smooth. Let cool slightly and glaze puffs. Yield: 2 dozen.

# PIES, TARTS, CUSTARDS, MOUSSES AND FROZEN DESSERTS

# CAFÉ AMERICAN STYLE

- The first records of coffee being consumed in North America were in 1668 and 1670, when William Penn wrote of buying green (coffee) beans in New York.

- Studies show that today's coffee drinkers on the East and West Coast and in larger metropolitan areas prefer darker roasts, while rural Americans prefer weaker, lighter brews.

- Cinnamon is a popular additive in Seattle.

- Macadamia nuts add flavor in Hawaii.

- Maple syrup is a special addition in Vermont.

- Philadelphians like cinnamon and cocoa in their coffee.

- Chicory is popular in New Orleans and Houston.

- Minnesotans have been known to mix eggshells and egg whites with coffee grounds.

- Flavored coffees, both regular and decaffeinated, are popular for after-dinner across the country.

- Hazelnut is most popular in California.

- Chocolate raspberry is a favorite in the South.

- Irish coffee is popular all along the Eastern seaboard.

- On a per capita basis, people living in Pittsburgh are said to drink more coffee than people in any other city in North America.

# MOCHA MACADAMIA NUT TART

By: **Frank Audino**
Wyndham Franklin Plaza

*3/4 cup granulated sugar*
*3 tablespoons brewed Melitta Premium coffee, cooled*
*1/3 cup light corn syrup*
*1/3 cup heavy cream*
*Pastry dough\**
*1 1/8 cups roasted macadamia nuts*
*coffee ice cream*

In a medium saucepan combine sugar, cooled coffee and corn syrup and bring to a boil. Cook undisturbed until mixture reaches the soft-ball stage (234° on a candy thermometer). Remove from heat and add cream in a slow steady stream. Set aside until ready to use.

Roll out pastry dough to 1/4 inch thickness and press into 3-inch tart pans. Place onto a baking sheet and bake in a pre-heated 375° oven 12 to 14 minutes, or until lightly browned. Let cool.

Crush or coarsely chop macadamia nuts and place about 1/3 cup in each pastry shell. Cover with 2 tablespoons of the sauce and bake in a 350° oven for 5 minutes. Remove from oven and drizzle with an additional tablespoon of the sauce. Bake 2 minutes longer and set aside to cool.

Serve warm or at room temperature with a scoop of coffee ice cream.

## * Pastry Dough:

*1/2 pound (2 sticks) unsalted butter*
*1/4 cup confectioners sugar*
*Pinch salt*
*1 cup all-purpose flour*
*2 egg yolks*

Cream together butter, sugar and salt until smooth. Add flour gradually; then egg yolks, one at a time until absorbed and blended. Pat into a flattened ball, wrap in foil or plastic wrap and chill overnight.

# COFFEE AND SWEET CHOCOLATE MOUSSE TART

By: **Gary Coyle and Colleen Winston**
Rittenhouse Hotel

## Macadamia Nut Crust:

*2 sticks unsalted butter*
*1/2 cup sugar*
*1 small egg*
*2 1/2 cups all-purpose flour*
*1 cup unsalted macadamia nuts, toasted and*
  *coarsely chopped*

Cream butter and sugar together, add egg and blend well. Stir in flour and nuts until dough comes together and forms a ball. Chill for 30 minutes. Remove and roll out on a lightly floured board to about 3/8 inch thick. Cut circles and press into six buttered 4-inch flan rings or one 9 or 10-inch ring (or pie pan). Place on parchment-lined baking sheet. Trim off excess dough and press a piece of heavy duty foil snugly into each shell. Bake in a 350° oven 6 minutes; remove foil and bake 5 to 10 minutes longer or until golden brown. Let cool.

## Coffee Chocolate Mousse:

*9 ounces semi-sweet chocolate, chopped*
*6 tablespoons unsalted butter*
*4 egg yolks*
*1/2 cup sugar*
*3 tablespoons strong brewed Melitta Premium coffee*
*1 cup heavy cream*

Melt chocolate and butter together until smooth. Set aside and let cool. Beat egg yolks and sugar until thick and light. Blend in cooled chocolate and coffee. Whip cream to soft peaks and fold in. Fill tart shells flush to top and smooth. Chill and cover with Chocolate Glaze.

## Chocolate Glaze:

*6 ounces bittersweet or semi-sweet chocolate, chopped*
*1 cup heavy cream*
*2 tablespoons strong brewed Melitta Premium coffee*

Bring heavy cream to a full boil. Pour over chocolate, add coffee and stir until smooth. Let cool for 10 minutes and spread over tart to glaze. Chill until set.

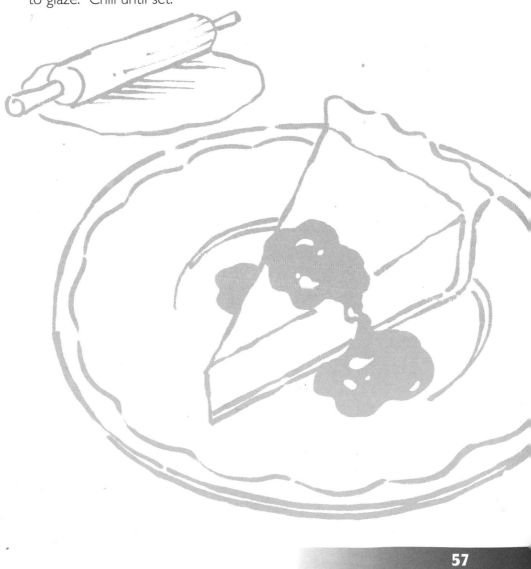

# MOCHA SILK PIE

*³/₄ cup butter*
*1 cup granulated sugar*
*2 eggs*
*3 squares (1 ounce each) unsweetened chocolate, melted and*
*cooled*
*3 tablespoons brewed Melitta Premium coffee, cooled*
*1 (6 ounce) prepared pie crust*
*1 cup sweetened whipped cream*
*Chocolate curls for garnish*

In a large bowl with mixer at medium speed, beat butter until light and fluffy. Add sugar; beat 2 minutes. Add eggs, one at a time, beating 3 minutes after each addition, scraping bowl occasionally.

Reduce speed to low. Pour melted chocolate and coffee in a thin stream into bowl, beating until blended. Increase speed to medium, beat 2 minutes until light and fluffy.

Spoon mixture into prepared pie crust, spreading evenly. Cover with plastic wrap. Refrigerate at least 4 hours or until filling is firm.

Decorate pie with whipped cream and garnish with chocolate curls. Makes 6 servings.

# MOCHA SPONGE CUSTARDS

*2 tablespoons butter*
*2/3 cup sugar*
*3 egg yolks*
*3 tablespoons all-purpose flour*
*2/3 cup strong brewed Melitta Premium coffee*
*2/3 cup milk*
*3 eggs whites, stiffly beaten*
*Sweetened whipped cream and coffee bean candies*

Preheat oven to 350°.  In a large bowl, using mixer at medium speed, beat butter and sugar for 2 minutes.  Add egg yolks; beat until thick, about 3 minutes more.

Using low speed, add flour alternately with coffee and milk.  Fold in beaten egg whites.

Divide batter among four buttered (8 ounce) ramekins, or six (6 ounce) custard cups.  Place ramekins in baking pan; add boiling water up to 1/2".

Bake 35 to 45 minutes or until set.  Serve hot or cold.  Garnish with whipped cream and coffee bean candies. Makes 4 to 6 servings.

# POACHED MOCHA TORTE WITH COFFEE-ROASTED BANANAS

By: **Eric Boerner**
Adam's Mark Hotel

## Poached Mocha Torte:

*6 ounces bittersweet or semi-sweet chocolate, chopped*
*6 ounces white chocolate, chopped*
*1 cup brewed Melitta Premium coffee, reduced to $^1/_3$ cup*
*3 large eggs*
*3 tablespoons Tia Maria or Kahlúa*

Melt chocolates together in a metal bowl or in top of a double boiler over boiling water. Combine coffee, eggs and coffee liqueur. Stir into melted chocolates. Pour into five small well-greased ramekins or soufflé cups. Place in a water bath and bake in a 325° oven for 1 hour, or until set. Cool 30 minutes and invert to remove from mold. Serve with Coffee Roasted Bananas, Cinnamon Caramel and/or Chocolate Sauces.

## Coffee-Roasted Bananas:

*1 cup Melitta Premium coffee grounds*
*$^1/_4$ cup water*
*2 large bananas*
*1 cup heavy cream*
*1 tablespoon sugar*
*$^1/_8$ teaspoon vanilla extract*

Combine coffee grounds and water to make a wet sand. Place bananas with the skins on in the middle of a sheet of aluminum foil and cover with coffee grounds. Seal package and roast in a 350° oven for 30 minutes. Remove bananas, brush off coffee grounds and scoop out pulp. Press through a sieve or puree and let cool. Whip cream with sugar and vanilla to soft peaks and fold in banana pulp. Serve with Mocha Torte that has been slightly warmed. Makes 5 servings.

## Cinnamon Caramel Sauce:

*½ cup light brown sugar*
*1 tablespoon light corn syrup*
*2 tablespoons unsalted butter*
*¼ cup heavy cream*
*2 tablespoons rum*
*pinch cinnamon*

Combine light brown sugar, corn syrup and butter and bring to a boil. Remove from heat and stir in remaining ingredients.

## Chocolate Sauce:

*¼ cup heavy cream*
*2 tablespoons Tia Maria or Kahlúa*
*2 ounces bittersweet or semi-sweet chocolate, chopped*

Bring cream and coffee liqueur to scalding. Pour over chocolate and stir until melted and smooth.

# BUDINO DI CAFÉ

By: **Lucia Ruggiero-Martella**

grano

*4 cups heavy cream*
*¼ cup strong brewed Melitta Premium coffee*
*2 tablespoons confectioners sugar*
*2 packages unflavored gelatin*

Place cream, coffee, sugar, and gelatin in a saucepan and bring to a boil. Simmer 10 to 15 minutes, remove from heat and let cool.

## Caramelized Sugar:

*1 cup sugar*
*½ cup water*
*2 drops lemon juice*

Bring sugar, water and lemon juice to a boil and continue cooking to soft ball stage (234°). Pour immediately into six or eight custard cups or soufflé molds and let set. Spoon in gelatin mixture and refrigerate until firm. To serve, unmold onto serving plates and serve with cooled Caramel Sauce.

## Caramel Sauce:

*½ cup sugar*
*¼ cup water*
*½ cup milk, heated*
*3 egg yolks*

Bring sugar and water to a boil and cook until light brown in color. Remove from heat, add warmed milk and bring to a boil. Gradually stir into egg yolks, whisking or beating well. Return to pan and cook on very low heat about 5 minutes. Do not boil.

# CAPPUCCINO GLACÉ

By: **Jodi Klocko**
Le Bec Fin

*2 whole eggs*
*5 egg yolks*
*½ cup sugar*
*¼ cup light corn syrup*
*1 tablespoon unflavored gelatin*
*3 tablespoons cold water*
*¼ teaspoon cinnamon*
*2 ounces semi-sweet chocolate, melted*
*¼ cup hazelnut liqueur*
*½ cup prepared Melitta Premium coffee extract\**
*2 cups heavy cream*
*1 tablespoon vanilla extract*

Blend together eggs, yolks, sugar and corn syrup in a bowl or in top of a double boiler. Whisk over barely simmering water until sugar is dissolved and mixture is warm to the touch. Remove and set aside.

Soften gelatin in cold water about 5 minutes. Place over simmering water to dissolve. Stir into egg mixture and transfer to a mixing bowl. Beat on medium-high speed until mixture cools and triples in volume. Add cinnamon and melted chocolate, blending well. Stir in hazelnut liqueur and coffee extract and mix completely.

Whip heavy cream to soft peaks, add vanilla and fold into chocolate mixture. Pour into a mold or a parchment or foil-lined loaf pan and freeze overnight. Let soften a few minutes, unmold, and slice to serve. Garnish as desired.

## * Coffee Extract:

*1 ½ cups boiling water*
*1 cup ground Melitta Premium coffee*

Pour boiling water over coffee, stir, and let steep for 5 minutes. Strain through a Melitta coffee filter or a fine strainer and set aside to cool.

# CHILLED MOCHA SOUFFLÉ

By: **Andrea Gibson**
  Splendido Bar and Grill

*8 ounces semi-sweet chocolate, chopped*
*1 ½ cups heavy cream*
*⅔ cup ground Melitta Premium coffee*
*4 egg yolks*
*¼ cup sugar*

Melt chocolate and set aside.

Combine cream and coffee and bring to a boil over medium heat. Remove from heat, cover, and allow to steep for 30 minutes. Strain and chill. Whip mixture until soft peaks form and set aside.

Beat egg yolks and sugar until light in color and thick. Blend in cooled chocolate. Stir in 1/3 of the whipped cream and coffee and fold in the rest. Spoon into soufflé dishes (with a collar, if desired) and place in freezer. Remove from freezer and refrigerate 20 to 30 minutes before serving. Unwrap collar, if using, and garnish as desired with whipped cream, chocolate coffee beans or cocoa powder. Makes 6 servings.

# FAT-FREE CHAMPAGNE AND COFFEE MOUSSE

By: **Peter Dierkes**
Pink Rose Pastry Shop

## Coffee Mousse:

*1 envelope unflavored gelatin*
*1 ¹/₄ cups sugar*
*1 ¹/₄ cups extra strong brewed Melitta Premium coffee*
*6 egg whites*
*Pinch salt*
*¹/₄ teaspoon almond extract*

Combine gelatin, sugar and cooled coffee in a saucepan. Heat until gelatin is dissolved. Cool and chill, stirring occasionally, until mixture starts to thicken. Whip egg whites until frothy and add salt. Beat to soft peaks, add almond extract and beat until stiff. Whip gelatin until frothy and fold in beaten whites. Let chill until mixture starts to thicken.

## Champagne Mousse:

*1 envelope gelatin*
*1 ¹/₄ cups sugar*
*³/₄ cup water*
*¹/₂ cup champagne or white wine*
*6 egg whites*
*pinch salt*

Put gelatin, sugar and water into a saucepan and stir until softened. Heat until gelatin is dissolved and remove from heat. Add champagne or wine and let cool. Chill, stirring occasionally until mixture starts to thicken. Whip egg whites until frothy, add salt and beat to firm peaks. Whip gelatin mixture until frothy and fold in beaten whites. Let chill until mixture starts to thicken.

## Assembly:

Spoon half of each mousse side by side in a serving bowl or in individual dessert dishes, wine glasses or chocolate cups. Let chill until completely set. To garnish, grate some chocolate over champagne mousse and top coffee mousse with espresso coffee beans. Makes 12-16 servings.

# MELITTA ENGLISH TRIFLE

*8 egg yolks*
*½ cup sugar*
*3 ¾ cups light cream - scalded*
*¼ cup extra strong brewed Melitta Premium coffee*
*½ teaspoon rum extract*
*1 teaspoon almond extract*
*Sponge cake or lady fingers*
*1 cup raspberry preserves*
*1 cup good quality sherry*
*2 packages lemon gelatin prepared with one package directions*
*1 cup of heavy cream - whipped*

In top of double boiler, beat yolks with sugar until thick. Slowly stir in scalded cream and coffee. Cook over simmering water, stirring constantly until thick. Remove from heat and stir in extracts. Let cool.

Line serving bowl with 1-inch thick layer of sponge cake or lady fingers. Spread with preserves. Sprinkle on sherry and let soak in. Spoon on alternate layers of mocha custard and chilled gelatin cut into cubes. Chill. Top with whipped cream. Decorate with candied cherries and almond slices.

# TIRAMISU

By: **Stanley Keenan**
Rittenhouse Hotel

*1 cup heavy cream*
*1 pound Mascarpone cheese*
*3 whole eggs*
*5 egg yolks*
*1 cup sugar*
*¼ cup water*
*2 teaspoons unflavored gelatin*
*¼ cup cold water*
*½ tablespoon ground Melitta Premium coffee*

Whip cream to soft peaks. Slowly blend in Mascarpone and set aside.
Beat eggs and yolks until double in volume. Heat sugar and 1/4 cup water or enough to cover and bring to a boil. Cook until soft ball stage (234°). Slowly pour hot sugar syrup into eggs while beating on low. Increase speed and continue beating until completely cooled.

Soften gelatin in remaining 1/4 cup water and heat to dissolve. Let cool slightly and blend into eggs. Fold in Mascarpone mixture and coffee granules and pour into ramekins, coffee cups or a mold. (Mold may be lined with ladyfingers, if desired.) Refrigerate or freeze until firm. To unmold, dip in warm water and turn out onto a serving dish. Serve with Melitta Coffee Anglaise.

## Melitta Coffee Anglaise:

*1 cup milk*
*1 cup heavy cream*
*½ vanilla bean, split or 1 teaspoon vanilla extract*
*6 egg yolks*
*½ cup sugar*
*1 cup brewed Melitta Premium coffee reduced to 2 tablespoons*

Combine milk, cream and vanilla bean (if using) and bring to a boil. Blend egg yolks and sugar and whisk until combined. Pour hot liquids into egg mixture while stirring. Return to heat and cook on low until sauce thickens enough to coat the back of a spoon. Cool over ice water, stirring occasionally. Add coffee, (vanilla extract if using) and strain.

# DOUBLE COFFEE GRANITA

By: **Andrea Damon Gibson**
  Splendido Bar and Grill

*2 cups ground Melitta Premium coffee*
*¹/₂ cup sugar*
*Zest 1 lemon, in strips*
*4 cups water*

Combine all ingredients in a saucepan and bring to a boil. Remove from heat, cover and let infuse for 30 minutes. Strain 3 to 4 times, place in shallow container and freeze. Stir every 20 minutes to create crystals until all liquid is frozen. Cover and store in freezer. Break up and serve in dessert dishes or stemmed glasses.
Makes 6-8 servings.

# SWEETHEART COFFEE MOLD

*1 envelope unflavored gelatin*
*1 cup light cream*
*2 (8 ounce) packages cream cheese, softened*
*⅓ cup sugar*
*1 cup strong brewed Melitta Premium coffee*
*2 tablespoons Amaretto Liqueur*
*Cocoa*

Lightly oil 1-quart heart-shaped mold.

In a small saucepan, sprinkle gelatin over cream. Let stand 5 minutes to soften. Over low heat, heat until gelatin is dissolved, stirring occasionally.

In a large bowl with a mixer at medium speed, beat cream cheese and sugar until light and fluffy. Reduce speed to low. Gradually beat in coffee, liqueur and gelatin mixture until well blended. Pour mixture into prepared mold. Cover with waxed paper. Refrigerate at least 6 hours.

Unmold onto serving plate. Sift cocoa over top. Garnish as desired. Makes 6 servings.

# QUICK AND EASY COFFEE DESSERTS

# COFFEE THROUGH THE YEARS

From the time 1300 years ago, when the Turks first cultivated coffee and made it their national beverage, the course of this remarkable beverage has flown freely through history, touching, if not always warming, the lives of the people who made it.

According to legend, it all began with a 9th Century goatherd named Khaldi. The behavior of his usually docile goats, Khaldi observed, changed to wild excitement whenever they partook of a strange berry, which grew wild in the fields. So the goatherd tried the berry himself, and suddenly became stimulated, clear-thinking and uncommonly happy.

From its discovery, whether by goatherd Khaldi or not, until the 16th Century, coffee belonged to Islam, where it was an enjoyable alternative to forbidden alcohol. Shunned at first by Christendom for its Muslim heritage, coffee eventually won the endorsement and blessing of Pope Clement VIII. Thus it began to flow through Europe with ringing testimonials from Voltaire, Rousseau, Robespierre, Napoleon and an American visitor to France, Benjamin Franklin.

Despite Franklin's endorsement, coffee got a cool reception early in American history. It was banned by the Puritans as a deterrent from work and prayer. But a century later, when tea literally fell from favor - to the bottom of Boston Harbor - coffee became the national beverage, a position it has never relinquished.

In the beginning of the 20th Century, a lady by the name of Melitta Bentz revolutionized the coffee industry by perfecting the "drip" method of coffeemaking, and since the early 1960s, Melitta's quest has been to bring a perfect cup of coffee to North American consumers.

But coffee is not only enjoyed as a hot or cold drink - it has other versatile uses. Our favorite is to use it as a dessert ingredient. We hope you'll enjoy some of our recipes, which we have collected over the years.

# CHILLED COFFEE SOUFFLÉ

*1 envelope unflavored gelatin*
*1 ¼ cups brewed Melitta Premium coffee*
*⅔ cups granulated sugar*
*dash salt*
*2 eggs, separated*
*1 cup whipping cream*

Soften gelatin in 1/4 cup cooled coffee. In a small saucepan, combine remaining 1 cup of coffee with sugar and salt. Add softened gelatin mixture and heat, stirring until sugar and gelatin are fully dissolved. Remove from heat and allow to cool. Beat egg yolks. Gradually stir cooled gelatin mixture into beaten egg yolks, and beat until foamy. Refrigerate until slightly thickened, but not firm.

Beat egg whites until stiff and gently fold into coffee mixture. Beat cream until stiff and fold into coffee mixture, combining well. Spoon into parfait glasses or a large serving dish and chill until firm. Top with whipped cream and toasted almonds, if desired. Serves 6.

# MOCHA NUT CAKE

*1/2 cup butter, room temperature*
*1 1/2 cups granulated sugar*
*3 eggs, separated*
*2 squares unsweetened chocolate, melted*
*2 cups all-purpose flour*
*1 tablespoon baking powder*
*1/4 teaspoon cream of tartar*
*1/2 teaspoon salt*
*3/4 cup milk*
*1/2 cup brewed Melitta Premium coffee*
*1 cup chopped walnuts*

Preheat oven to 350°. Cream butter until light. Gradually beat in sugar and egg yolks. Blend in melted chocolate. In a separate bowl, sift together flour, baking powder, cream of tartar and salt. Add dry ingredients to creamed mixture, alternately with milk and coffee. Beat egg whites until stiff and fold in with nuts.

Divide batter between two 8-inch round cake pans (grease and flour or line the bottoms only). Bake for 30 to 35 minutes. Remove from pans and cool on racks.

## Rich Mocha Frosting

*6 tablespoons butter*
*3 cups sifted confectioners sugar*
*1/2 cup cocoa*
*1/2 cup strong brewed cold Melitta Premium coffee*
*1 teaspoon vanilla extract*

Beat butter until light. Sift confectioners sugar with cocoa and add gradually to beaten butter, alternating with coffee. Add vanilla and beat until smooth and light. Spread between cool cake layers and over top and sides.

# COFFEE CUSTARD BRULEÉ

*2 cups heavy cream*
*1 cup strong brewed Melitta Premium coffee*
*⅓ cup granulated sugar*
*3 eggs*
*3 egg yolks*
*1 teaspoon vanilla extract*
*⅔ cup brown sugar*

Over moderate heat, stir sugar until dissolved in cream and coffee. Remove from heat and allow to cool. Blend together whole eggs and egg yolks. Stir cooled coffee mixture into egg mixture. Add vanilla and whisk lightly to blend. Pour into shallow baking dish or individual ovenproof custard cups.

Set baking dish or custard cups in a larger pan of hot water and bake at 300° for 35 to 45 minutes, until center of custard is just firm. Be careful not to overcook. Remove from oven and let cool. Chill until ready to serve.

Before serving, sift brown sugar evenly over custard surface. Place baking dish or dishes as close as possible to the broiling element and watching carefully, broil until the brown sugar is melted. Be careful not to burn the sugar. Remove from oven and chill until serving time. Makes 6 servings.

# COFFEE SPONGE CAKE

*5 eggs, separated*
*5 tablespoons cold brewed Melitta Premium coffee*
*1 cup granulated sugar*
*1 teaspoon vanilla extract*
*1 cup all-purpose flour*
*1 teaspoon cream of tartar*
*Dash salt*

Combine egg yolks, cold coffee and sugar and beat until very light and lemon colored (about 5 minutes with an electric mixer). Fold in vanilla and flour, combining well. Beat egg whites until foamy. Add cream of tartar and salt and beat until stiff. Fold into flour mixture.

Pour into ungreased 10-inch tube pan and bake in a 300° oven for 70 minutes. Invert on rack to cool. Serve with Coffee Pecan Sauce.

## Coffee Pecan Sauce:

*1 cup corn syrup*
*1 1/2 cups strong brewed Melitta coffee, cooled*
*3 tablespoons cornstarch*
*2 tablespoons butter*
*1 teaspoon vanilla*
*1/2 cup pecan halves*

In a small saucepan over medium heat, blend together corn syrup, coffee and cornstarch. Cook, stirring until thickened and smooth. Stir in butter, vanilla and pecans. Serve hot or cold, over cake. Serves 6-8.

# BANANA FLAMBÉ

*2 ripe bananas*
*1 tablespoon lemon juice*
*2 tablespoons butter*
*¼ cup brown sugar*
*¼ cup hot, freshly brewed Melitta Premium coffee*
*¼ cup white rum*
*Small container vanilla ice cream*

Peel bananas and cut into 1/2 inch slices. Brush each with lemon juice to avoid discoloration. Melt butter and brown sugar in a frying pan. Add bananas and cook over medium heat until tender. Stir in hot coffee and remove from heat. Warm rum slightly, ignite and pour over bananas, basting until flame dies. Serve immediately over vanilla ice cream. Serves 4.

# MELITTA TRUFFLES

*⅔ cup butter*
*2 cups sifted confectioners sugar*
*6 squares semi-sweet chocolate, melted and cooled*
*3 tablespoons strong brewed Melitta Premium coffee*
*1 teaspoon rum*
*1 ¼ cup chocolate wafer crumbs*

Thoroughly cream butter and sugar and add melted chocolate. Add coffee and rum and mix well. Chill for 3 to 4 hours, until mixture is firm enough to handle. Drop mixture by small teaspoonfuls into crumbs and form into balls. Roll each in crumbs until well coated. Chill for at least 2 hours before serving. Store in refrigerator, tightly covered. Makes approximately 50 truffles.

# MELITTA NUGGETS

*½ cup butter, room temperature*
*¾ cup brown sugar*
*1 egg, beaten*
*1 ¼ cups all-purpose flour*
*½ teaspoon each of cinnamon, baking soda, allspice, nutmeg,*
*ground cloves and salt*
*¼ cup brewed Melitta Premium coffee, cooled*
*1 cup raisins*
*½ cup chopped walnuts*

Preheat oven to 350°. Cream butter. Gradually beat in brown sugar and egg. In a separate bowl, sift together flour, cinnamon, baking soda, allspice, nutmeg, cloves and salt. Add to creamed mixture and stir in coffee, raisins and walnuts. Combine well.

Drop from a teaspoon onto a greased baking sheet and bake for 10 to 12 minutes. Remove from pan with a spatula and cool on wire racks. Makes approximately 40 cookies.

# CREAMY COFFEE FUDGE

*2 cups granulated sugar*
*1 cup strong brewed Melitta Premium coffee, cooled*
*1 tablespoon butter*
*¼ teaspoon cream of tartar*
*Dash salt*
*1 cup chopped walnuts or pecans*

In a saucepan over moderate heat, mix together all ingredients except nuts, stirring until sugar is dissolved. Boil, stirring constantly until mixture reaches the soft ball stage (234°). Remove from heat and cool to lukewarm without stirring. Beat until mixture thickens and is no longer glossy. Stir in nuts and pour into buttered pie plate or dish, to a thickness of approximately 1 inch. Refrigerate until firm. Cut into serving pieces. Quantity varies with thickness of fudge.

# FROZEN CHOCOLATE CAPPUCCINO MOUSSE

*1 quart chocolate ice cream*
*¹/₂ cup brewed extra-strong Melitta Premium coffee*
*¹/₂ cup granulated sugar*
*4 large egg yolks*
*2 tablespoons coffee-flavored liqueur*
*¹/₂ teaspoon ground cinnamon*
*2 cups whipped cream*
*Whipped cream and fancy cookies for garnish*

Place ice cream in refrigerator to soften, about 30 minutes. In a saucepan over medium heat, bring coffee and sugar to a boil. Boil 4 minutes. Place egg yolks in a small mixer bowl. With mixer at medium speed, add hot coffee mixture in a thin stream, beating until yolks are thick, pale lemon-colored and cooled, about 3 minutes. Beat in liqueur and cinnamon; pour into large bowl.

Fold whipped cream into coffee mixture and divide between two 8-inch loaf pans. Randomly spoon ice cream into mousse mixture in pans. Cover with plastic wrap; freeze until firm, at least 6 hours.

Scoop into dessert goblets. Garnish with whipped cream and fancy cookies. Makes 8 servings.

# INTERNATIONAL COFFEES, FAVORITE COFFEE DRINKS AND DESSERT DRINKS

# QUICK TIPS

- Store coffee in an airtight container and keep it cool. The refrigerator is best. Use the freezer for long-term storage.

- Cafe Amaretto is an elegant drink that's a snap to make. Just add one-to-two tablespoons of almond liqueur and one teaspoon of brown sugar to each cup of regular strength coffee. Float a dollop of whipped cream on top.

- Cold coffee is a tasty alternative to wine in most dessert recipes.

- For a fast Mocha Shake, blend together a cup of cold coffee, and a spoonful of chocolate ice cream.

- Make refreshing Vienna Iced Coffee by stirring softened vanilla ice cream into glasses of cold coffee.

- Use leftover coffee as half the liquid in your next beef stew. Nice flavor. Or, replace all the liquid with coffee.

- Freeze leftover coffee in ice cube trays and use coffee cubes with regular strength coffee. No more diluted iced coffee!

- Need a special way to entertain quickly? Set up a coffee bar. Brew fresh Melitta coffee and let your guests select flavorings and condiments to dress-up their coffees. Include liqueurs or non-alcoholic flavorings, whipped cream, chocolate shavings and anything else you think would be fun!

- For a small amount of coffee required for some recipes, brew a small amount with a Melitta one-cup filter cone. It's quick, inexpensive and saves on coffee.

## Espresso Coffee:

Fill espresso cups with freshly brewed espresso coffee. Add sugar, if desired, twist of lemon peel and serve.

## Cappuccino:

Combine equal quantities of steaming espresso and steaming milk. Pour into cappuccino cups and sprinkle with cinnamon and nutmeg.

## Chocolaccino:

Prepare as above but serve in full-size cups (mug), top with whipped cream and a mound of shaved French Chocolate.

## Spiced Coffee Vienna:

Combine 3 cups of very hot, extra strength coffee over 2 cinnamon sticks and 4 whole cloves. Let stand over lowest heat for 10 to 15 minutes. Strain. Pour into wine glasses and top with softly whipped cream. Sprinkle with nutmeg and serve with sugar. Makes 6 servings.

## Viennese Coffee Frost:

Brew 6 cups espresso or double-strength coffee. While it is still hot, pour over 4 crushed cinnamon sticks, 3 cloves and 8 allspice berries. After an hour, strain and pour over ice in tall glasses. Sweeten to taste and top with whipped cream. Makes 4 servings.

# Belgian Coffee:

Beat 1 egg white until stiff. Add 1/4 teaspoon vanilla to 1/2 cup heavy cream and whip. Fold into egg white. Fill coffee cups 1/3 full with cream mixture. Fill with hot coffee. Serve at once. Sweeten to taste. Makes 4 servings.

# Irish Coffee:

Into a warmed wine glass, place 2 teaspoons of sugar and fill glass about 2/3 with hot coffee. Add about 2 tablespoons of Irish whiskey, stir and top with softly whipped cream. Makes 1 serving.

# Latin Coffee El Salvador:

Fill electric blender container half full of finely chopped ice. Add 1-1/2 cups cool espresso coffee and 1 tablespoon sugar. Blend until thick and foamy. Pour into 4 tall glasses.

# Iced Coffee Rio:

Prepare 5 tablespoons fine grind coffee with 3 cups water. Chill coffee until very cold. Whip 1 cup heavy cream with 2 tablespoons sugar until it holds a firm shape. Put 1 scoop of vanilla ice cream and 1 ounce of coffee liqueur in each of 4 glasses. Fill the remainder of the glass with the coffee. Top with additional whipped cream and serve immediately.

# FAVORITE COFFEE DRINKS

## Minted Mocha Mist:

In a pitcher, stir together 1 cup chilled Melitta coffee and 3 ounces chocolate mint liqueur. Pour into tall glasses filled with ice cubes. Add heavy cream to taste. Garnish with a fresh mint sprig and enjoy!

## Coffee Grog:

Combine peels of 1 orange and 1 lemon, cut in strips, 4 cinnamon sticks (each about 3 inches long), 1-1/2 teaspoons whole cloves, 1/3 cup sugar, 1/4 cup chocolate syrup, 1/2 teaspoon anise flavoring and 2 quarts strong hot coffee in large carafe or deep chafing dish. Steep over very low heat for 15 minutes (do not boil). Serve in demitasses, cups or small mugs, with a twist of lemon peel and a spoonful of whipped cream. Makes about 12 half-cup servings.

## Coffee Banana:

Slice 2 ripe bananas into an electric blender. Add 1/2 pint (1 cup) coffee ice cream, 1/2 cup light cream, 1/4 teaspoon almond extract, 1/2 teaspoon lemon juice and 1 tablespoon sugar. Blend until thick and fluffy. Pour into 2 tall glasses. Serve at once, or chill until ready to serve.

## Coffee De Cacao:

Use creme de cacao, extra-strength ice cold coffee and whipped cream. Pour 2 tablespoons creme de cacao in bottom of wine glass. Fill almost to top with strong, ice cold coffee. Mix. Float softly whipped cream on top. Makes 1 serving.

## Chilled Coffee A la Crème:

Fill parfait glasses to the brim with chipped ice. Pour in extra-strength cold coffee, sweetened or not, filling glasses about 2/3 full. If desired, add a dash of liqueur or brandy, such as Anisette, Cointreau, Cognac, Kümmel, Grand Marnier, Maraschino or White Creme de Menthe. Pour in plain, heavy cream almost to brim. Serve at once.

## Coffee Velvet:

1 quart vanilla ice cream, 6 cups hot, double-strength coffee and whipped cream. Place 1 large scoop of vanilla ice cream in each of 6 tall glasses. Pour hot, double-strength coffee carefully over ice cream until glass is about 2/3 full. Add a second scoop of ice cream and fill glass with coffee. Garnish with whipped cream and add a sprinkle of nutmeg if desired. You will need long spoons for the first half of this dessert-beverage, but you will drink the latter half.

# DESSERT DRINKS

## Monte Carlo

*1/2 cup heavy or whipping cream*
*2 teaspoons brandy, warmed*
*4 teaspoons granulated sugar*
*1/2 cup brandy, warmed*
*2 cups hot, freshly brewed Melitta Premium coffee*
*4 scoops vanilla ice cream*
*1/4 cup coffee liqueur*
*2 tablespoons green creme de menthe*
*Garnish: red or green cherries, optional*

Whip cream until stiff. Pour 1/2 teaspoon warmed brandy into each of 4 mugs or heavy stemmed glasses and swirl to moisten insides. Add a teaspoon of sugar to each glass/mug and rotate to evenly coat insides. Pour 2 tablespoons warmed brandy into each glass. Carefully ignite each with match, rotating glasses until flames burn out. Half fill each glass with hot, freshly brewed Melitta coffee. Add a scoop of ice cream; then top with chilled whipped cream and drizzle with green creme de menthe. Add cherries if you wish and serve at once. Makes 4 servings.

## Crème de Café

*1/4 cup coffee liqueur*
*1/4 cup white creme de menthe*
*1 1/2 cups hot, freshly brewed Melitta Premium coffee*
*Whipped cream and shaved chocolate garnish*

Combine the coffee liqueur and creme de menthe and divide equally between 2 large mugs. Fill both with hot, freshly brewed Melitta coffee. Top with whipped cream and chocolate shavings and enjoy immediately. Serves 2.

# Apricot Coffee Cream

*2 cups brewed Melitta Premium coffee, cooled*
*2 10 ounce cans apricot nectar*
*2 cups coffee ice cream, softened*
*¼ cup granulated sugar*
*1 cup milk*
*½ teaspoon almond extract*

Place coffee, apricot nectar, ice cream and sugar in blender or mixer. Blend/mix for 30 seconds. Add milk and almond extract and blend well. Serve at once in tall glasses. Makes 6 servings.

# COFFEE BREWING TIPS

*Melitta*

The best way to enjoy a great dessert is with a great cup of coffee, starting with Melitta coffee. But in order to get the best flavor and taste, follow these easy brewing tips.

1. Make sure the coffee grind is compatible with your coffeemaker. Use extra fine grind Melitta Premium coffee with cone drip coffeemakers.

2. Start with a clean coffeemaker. Hard water leaves sediments that can affect taste. To avoid this problem, clean and rinse your carafe or coffeemaker after each use and use Melitta descaler at least once a month.

3. Use the freshest ground coffee or beans available. Melitta's vacuum packed ground coffee assures optimum freshness.

4. Measure carefully. With the Melitta system, use 2 teaspoons or one Melitta scoop of fine grind coffee to each 6 oz of water. For coarser grinds, double the coffee quantity.

5. Always use fresh cold water for filtering — artificially softened water can affect taste.

6. Brew carefully. With a manual cone filter system, remove boiled water from heat a few seconds before pouring. First moisten the grounds with the boiled water and allow to soak for a few minutes, to assure release of the full coffee flavor. Then, gently add the rest of the water.

7. Make only as much coffee as you need. Never reheat cold coffee and never boil brewed coffee.

8. Store coffee in an airtight container and keep it cold. The refrigerator is best. Use the freezer for long term storage.